Crooked Line
Citizen A

Crooked Line

Crooked line

Citizen A

Publisher

Amazon

ISBN: 978-0-620-66400-4

Dedicated to all the disappointed South African Citizens

who after being fed with false hope, still hope for

the reality of a Prosperous Country for all.

This is a book about a Promised Land that never materialised.

A false hope waved in front of a good and decent people by a group hungry for power. This is indeed an attempt to slightly expose the present ANC - which although they did not start off corrupt - yet became corrupt.

Maybe it is a wake-up call to some South Africans –

hopefully it will affect most people!

"Not to oppose error, is to approve it;

And not to defend truth, is to suppress it"

Pope St. Felix III

Contents

"One of the penalties for refusing to participate in politics is that you end up being governed by your inferiors." – Plato.

This age-old truth is still so relevant today when one hears many people say they are not interested in politics. The fact which most of these people ignore, seems to be that the power to govern then stays in the hands of those less qualified to rule. This exactly is so clearly visible today. Surely qualification means a lot more than education in this context. How long must the people stand on the side-lines and be content to receive the scraps the tyrants will keep throwing at them? If we decide to stay on the pavilion, watching politicians wasting our resources no-one else will step in! They will continue to destroy the fortunes of our land and the future of our generations to come. Let us restore our own power! Martin Luther King Junior said, "there is no bigger tragedy than when a people sleep through a revolution". May this small work succeed in revealing the facts as to stir the spirit of the people to radical action.

In Crooked line the author attempts to make clear the obvious. A line when not drawn straight should not be considered a line; it becomes instead a curve, a bend, a twist, a turn, a bow, a corner, a stoop or just plain a crook. Since we have followed this skew line for more than twenty years with the hope that it will become a straight line, we shall call it a line, but as it appears: crooked. Hence the Crooked Line refers to what is supposed to be a line, but those drawing the line made it skew. Perhaps the ANC government attempted a straight line, particularly under the presidency of Nelson Mandela or even way back under the Reverend Ntuli's Leadership.

What happened since then? What happened to moral government, statesmanship and integrity in leaders? Were those in current leadership perhaps staggering under the drunken stupor of newfound power and wealth? Were they so unstable that the line became as twisted as it is today. Do we have any hope of this line being repaired or do we need the eraser of a revolution to commence the drawing of a new line?

Crooked Line will attempt to awaken the sleeping, yet powerful, force of a people who were on the receiving end of wrongdoing. We must awake and acknowledge that which we are offered by the present Government is not what we were promised. We need drastic action, and real change to participate in the land of promise. The Line which had been crookedly drawn by so called Architects of a Country that never materialized must be replaced by a new straight line. This is important to all in this beautiful Land called South Africa. Everyone should be living and treated as equals.

"Becoming part of the newly democratic public service after 1994, had nothing to do with self-service, political-party centred occupation, positions of power or about using those positions for the accumulation of personal and/or family wealth" says Doctor McKinley. They viewed this as an opportunity to replace a dishonest civic service representing only a small minority with a more representative sector. South Africans in service that would be rising above private interest to serve the needs of the people by corporative and individual actions. Selfless efforts driven by ethical moralities that would show the legitimacy of the Public sector, as mandated by the people.

Why an insurgence or revolution you may ask. It was justifiably said that drastic actions call for drastic measures. The way of the Crooked Line is definitely drastic. It mockingly cuts through the hunger, homeless, unemployed masses and only insultingly shows temporary kindness during the short season prior to an Election, as again it took a sharp bend. After Elections, it goes back to stealing, lying, corruption, and self-enrichment. The drastic ways in which the people are ignored, and left to suffer calls for an equal return of force. Let the People indeed govern as it was pledged.

The African National Congress had been in power in South Africa since 1994 when the late Nelson Mandela became the first democratically elected President of the Country. Much promises were made and today, most South African citizens feel let down as promises made by the government of their choosing, still seems derailed or deferred twenty-one years later. In fact, for most South Africans life had become worst instead of better.   One of the liberties inscribed in the Freedom Charter of the African National Congress (as based upon the will of all the people) proclaims, "The People Shall Govern". I must ask, is this how the People govern?

Many freedom fighters, on both sides of the fence, are left behind disillusioned and disappointed whilst a few politicians have become the wealthy, arrogant, selfish minority. This happens at the expense of needs, such as proper housing, food, employment, and the list goes on. Many can be heard whispering the dreadful wish that the old regime was better. "Freedom cannot be eaten or cover our heads", has become the new cry of the people.

As the twenty-one years continue to empower politicians, the nation becomes used to a sub-standard lifestyle. The Country's Economy continues to drop to a record low. Living for ordinary South Africans became tough as most now find themselves either under the Breadline or struggling to stay above it. Inflation soars with continuous price increases, from fuel to food. Those who had the aspiration to rise against the status quo, either became exhausted for standing alone, or got bought over by those against development posing as protectors of democracy and the rights of the people.

How much time is required to "erase the injustices of the past"? If twenty-one years were not enough, will forty-two years be? Shall the people wait indefinitely for the life they were promised, which has become the privilege of a few? Is time really the issue preventing the people from enjoying life in their Country of residence? Is it really true that more time is needed or is it merely once again a promise without a deadline? Forgetting that if it cannot expire, it does not mean that it will be forgotten. Unfulfilled promises are equal to lies and lying has a short lifespan.

Crooked Line is written about these promises made to a people who were believing and expecting. Most of whom shed blood, tears and sweat to win a democracy. People who had the tenacity and determination to come against a previous government who abused, insulted and mistreated them. This is a cry to the same citizens to rise once again. Rise and resist the flood of injustice, dressed up in democracy and hiding behind an old dress called the past. Heed the words of the late Nelson Mandela, ".....when the ANC Government does to you, what the Apartheid Regime did to you, then you must do to the ANC government what you did to the Apartheid Government". After more than twenty years, it is indeed time to fight for a better life for all. Let us rise and redraw the Crooked Line straight. Our Country deserves better? South Africans need better.

The Freedom Charter is incorporated in the Addendum to help us see how unfulfilled promises were made to everyone. They were and still are not unattainable as it was realised for a minority. A few fortunate politicians and their families benefitted from the fight for a better life. For the rest of the Country: The Struggle continues. It becomes urgent to create a Straight Line from this Crooked.

Chapter 1

The Crooked Line of Apartheid

A Historical view

'It is essential to peep into the windows of the past in order to view the present and future properly so as to not repeat the mistakes of the past.'

Apartheid was the system of racial segregation in South Africa enforced through legislation by the National Party (NP), the governing party from 1948 to 1994. Under apartheid, the rights, associations, and movements of the majority black inhabitants and other ethnic groups were curtailed and Afrikaner minority rule was maintained. Apartheid was developed after World War II by the Afrikaner-dominated National Party and BroederBond organizations. The ideology was also enforced in the then South West Africa, which was administered by South Africa under a League of Nations mandate (revoked in 1966 via United Nations Resolution 2145) until it gained independence as Namibia in 1990. By extension, the term is currently used for forms of systematic segregation, established by the state authority in a country, against the social and civil rights of a certain group of citizens, due to ethnic prejudices.

Racial segregation in South Africa began in colonial times under the Dutch Empire, until 1795 when the British took over the Cape of Good Hope. Apartheid as an officially structured policy was introduced after the general election of 1948. Legislation classified inhabitants into four racial groups—"black", "white", "coloured", and "Indian", the last two of which were divided into several sub-classifications [8].

Residential areas were segregated. From 1960 to 1983, 3.5 million non-white South Africans were removed from their homes, and forced into segregated neighbourhoods, in one of the largest mass removals in modern history. Non-white political representation was abolished in 1970. Starting in that year black people were deprived of their citizenship, legally becoming citizens of one of ten tribally based self-governing homelands called Bantustans. Four of these homelands became nominally independent states. The government segregated education, medical care, beaches, and other public services, and provided black people with services that were often inferior to those of white people.

Apartheid sparked significant internal resistance and violence, and a long arms and trade embargo against South Africa. Since the 1950s, a series of popular uprisings and protests was met with the banning of opposition and imprisoning of anti-apartheid leaders. As unrest spread and became more effective and militarised, state organisations responded with repression and violence. Along with the sanctions placed on South Africa by the international community, this made it increasingly difficult for the government to maintain the regime. Apartheid reforms in the 1980s failed to quell the mounting opposition. During 1990 President Frederik Willem de Klerk began negotiations to end apartheid. This culminated in multi-racial democratic elections in 1994, won by the African National Congress under Nelson Mandela. The vestiges of apartheid still shape South African politics and society. De Klerk began the process of dismantling apartheid with the release of Mandela's mentor and several other political prisoners in October 1989. Although the official abolition of apartheid occurred in 1991 with repeal of the last of the remaining apartheid laws, non-whites were not allowed to vote until 1993 and the end of apartheid is widely regarded as arising from the 1994 national elections.

Chapter 2

Crooked becoming straight

Straightening a line which had been skew for so many years is never easy. It calls for strong leadership, integrity and altruism. To make it run straight requires sacrifice, compromise and greatness. Are there still South Africans around who possess those qualities or are they extinct?

Apartheid was dismantled in a series of negotiations from 1990 to 1993, culminating in elections in 1994, the first in South Africa with universal suffrage.

From 1990 to 1996 apartheid as a legal instrument was abolished. This was earnestly begun, with two meetings between the Nationalist government. The ANC began negotiations in 1990, in order to prepare the way for talks towards a peaceful transition of power. These meetings were successful in laying down the preconditions for negotiations – despite the considerable tensions still abounding within the country.

At the first meeting, the NP and ANC discussed the conditions for negotiations. The meeting was held at Groote Schuur, the president's official residence. They released the Groote Schuur Minute, which stated that before negotiations commenced political prisoners would be freed and all exiles allowed to return.

There were fears that the change of power would be violent. To avoid this, it was essential that a peaceful resolution between all parties be reached. In December 1991, the Convention for a Democratic South Africa (CODESA) began negotiations on the formation of a multiracial transitional government and a new constitution extending political rights to all groups. CODESA adopted a Declaration of Intent and committed itself to an "undivided South Africa".

Reforms and negotiations to end apartheid led to a backlash among the right-wing white opposition, leading to the Conservative Party winning a few by-elections against NP candidates. De Klerk responded by calling a whites-only referendum in March 1992 to decide whether negotiations should continue. A sixty-eight per cent majority gave its support. The victory instilled in De Klerk and the government a lot more confidence, giving the NP a stronger position in negotiations.

When negotiations resumed in May 1992, under the tag of CODESA II, stronger demands were made. The ANC and the government could not reach a compromise on how power should be shared during the transition to democracy. The NP wanted to retain a strong position in a transitional government, and the power to change decisions made by parliament.

Persistent violence added to the tension during the negotiations. This was due mostly to the intense rivalry between the Inkatha Freedom Party (IFP) and the ANC and the eruption of some traditional tribal and local rivalries between the Zulu and Xhosa historical tribal affinities, especially in the Southern Natal provinces. Although Mandela and Buthelezi met to settle their differences, they could not stem the violence. One of the worst cases of ANC-IFP violence was the Boipatong massacre of 17 June 1992, when 200 IFP militants attacked the Gauteng township of Boipatong, killing forty-five. Witnesses said the men arrived in police vehicles, supporting claims that elements within the police and army contributed to the ongoing violence. Subsequent judicial inquiries found the evidence of the witnesses to be unreliable or discredited, and that there was no evidence of National Party or police involvement in the massacre. When De Klerk visited the scene of the incident he was initially warmly welcomed, but he was suddenly confronted by a crowd of protesters brandishing stones and placards. The motorcade sped from the scene as police tried to hold back the crowd. Shots were fired by the police, and the PAC stated that three of its supporters had been gunned down. Nonetheless, the Boipatong massacre offered the ANC a pretext to engage in politics. Mandela argued that De Klerk, as head of state, was responsible for bringing an end to the carnage. He also accused the South African police of inciting the ANC-IFP violence. This formed the basis for ANC's withdrawal from the negotiations, and the CODESA forum broke down completely at this stage.

The Bisho butchery on 7 September 1992 brought matters to a head. The Ciskei Defence Force killed twenty-nine people and injured 200 when they opened fire on ANC marchers demanding the reincorporation of the Ciskei homeland into South Africa. In the aftermath, Mandela and De Klerk agreed to meet to find ways to end the spiralling violence. This led to a continuation of negotiations.

Right-wing violence also added to the hostilities of this period. The assassination of Chris Hani on 10 April 1993 threatened to plunge the country into chaos. Hani, the popular general secretary of the South African Communist Party (SACP), was assassinated in 1993 in Dawn Park in Johannesburg by Janusz Waluś, an anti-communist Polish refugee who had close links to the white nationalist Afrikaner Weerstandsbeweging (AWB). Hani enjoyed widespread support beyond his constituency in the SACP and ANC. He was regarded as a potential successor to Mandela; his death brought forth protests throughout the country and across the international community, but ultimately proved a turning point, after which the main parties pushed for a settlement with increased determination. On 25 June 1993, the AWB used an armoured vehicle to crash through the doors of the Kempton Park World Trade Centre where talks were still going ahead under the Negotiating Council, though this did not derail the process.

In addition to the continuing "black-on-black" violence, there were a number of attacks on white civilians by the PAC's military wing, the Azanian People's Liberation Army (APLA). The PAC was hoping to strengthen their standing by attracting the support of the angry, impatient youth. In the St James Church massacre on 25 July 1993, members of the APLA opened fire in a church in Cape Town, killing eleven members of the congregation and wounding fifty-eight.

In 1993 De Klerk and Mandela were jointly awarded the Nobel Peace Prize "for their work for the peaceful termination of the apartheid regime, and for laying the foundations for a new democratic South Africa"

Violence persisted right up to the 1994 elections. Lucas Mangope, leader of the Bophuthatswana homeland, declared that it would not take part in the elections. It had been decided that, once the temporary constitution had come into effect, the homelands would be incorporated into South Africa, but Mangope did not want this to happen. There were strong protests against his decision, leading to a coup d'état in Bophuthatswana on 10 March which deposed Mangope, despite the intervention of white right-wingers hoping to maintain him in power. Three AWB militants were killed during this intervention, and harrowing images were shown on national television and in newspapers across the world.

Two days before the elections, a car bomb exploded in Johannesburg, killing nine people. The day before the elections, another went off, injuring thirteen. At midnight on 26–27 April 1994 the old flag was struck and the old (now co-official) national anthem Die Stem ("The Call") was sung, followed by the hoisting of the new rainbow flag and singing of the other co-official anthem, Nkosi Sikelel' iAfrika ("God Bless Africa").

Chapter 3

Freedom won!

Early in 1989, Botha suffered a stroke; he was prevailed upon to resign in February 1989. He was succeeded as president later that year by FW de Klerk. Despite his initial reputation as a conservative, De Klerk moved decisively towards negotiations to end the political stalemate in the country. In his opening address to parliament on 2 February 1990, De Klerk announced that he would repeal discriminatory laws and lift the 30-year ban on leading anti-apartheid groups such as the African National Congress, the Pan Africanist Congress, the South African Communist Party (SACP) and the United Democratic Front. The Land Act was ended. De Klerk also made his first public commitment to release Nelson Mandela, to return to press freedom and to suspend the death penalty. Media restrictions were lifted and political prisoners not guilty of common-law crimes were released.

On 11 February 1990, Nelson Mandela was released from Victor Verster Prison after more than twenty-seven years of confinement.

Having been instructed by the UN Security Council to end its long-standing involvement in South-West Africa / Namibia, and in the face of military stalemate in Southern Angola, and an escalation in the size and cost of the combat with the Cubans, the Angolans, and SWAPO forces and the growing cost of the border war, South Africa negotiated a change of control; Namibia became independent on 21 March 1990. The election was held on 27 April 1994 and went off peacefully throughout the country as twenty million South Africans cast their votes. There was some difficulty in organising the voting in rural areas, but people waited patiently for many hours to vote amidst a palpable feeling of goodwill. An extra day was added to give everyone the chance to make their choice known.

The ANC won 62.65 per cent of the National Vote and Nelson Mandela was sworn in as South Africa's president. The Government of National Unity was established, its cabinet made up of twelve ANC representatives, six from the NP, and three from the IFP. Thabo Mbeki and De Klerk were made deputy presidents.

The anniversary of the elections, 27 April, is celebrated as a public holiday known as Freedom Day.

Chapter 4

Democracy and Elections

The Oxford Dictionary defines democracy as follows: "A system of government by the whole population or all the eligible members of a state, typically through elected representatives".

Simon Kabanda in writing on African Democracy talks about "African standards for democracy". We surely have seen democracy in its alien forms in Africa. Why democracy does adjust its meaning when it is used on the African continent is not strange anymore. Kabanda names as examples African Countries like Kenya, Zambia and Zimbabwe where constitution-making processes have started democratically, but have broken down in the long run. South Africa has indeed joined that list. Why constitution-making processes?

It forms the basis for guiding democracy for any Country. However, the biggest challenge had been to follow the letter of the word. One must agree with Kabanda when he says that "Elections are one way through which people of a given country participate in governance and that Periodic elections are thus understood to be one of the pillars of democracy". "Elections as a pillar of democracy" he says, "should serve to promote and strengthen Democracy", but in Africa instead it has become a source of conflict. South Africa has definitely been suppressing that fact very well.

There are rumours of a clandestine delegation formed by the ANC in 1993. Men like Trevor Manuel, William Madushe and others were in this group. Their task was to devise a plan that would ensure the African National Congress would remain in power once they won the first election in 1994. This was relayed to me in the running up to the 2014 General Elections. After this conversation, I understood the statement of President Jacob Zuma when he claimed that "the ANC will rule until the Jesus returns". How is it that in several at random conversations with South African Voters, a ratio of seven out of ten denied having voted for the "ruling party"? Yet the ANC has not lost an election since 1994. How can the party who controls and owns the Independent Election Committee (IEC), ever lose an election? The plan devised by this group of ANC delegates, is paying off indeed.

Controlling all organs of state including the latter, is the result not understandable and expected? Is the South African president and government then not quite at liberty to mock its citizens, steal from and lie to them?

There are certainly better systems in the progressing age of technological advancement. There are ways to hold elections free and fair and prevent even the rumours of rigging or stealing an election. Why have these options never been explored and tested? New systems, structures and laws are definitely required to ensure that the will of the people succeeds. Or indeed democracy shall remain a foreign concept in South Africa, and perhaps for Africa as a continent.

The big question is whether a people who had never experienced the freedom that had now befall them, was ready for their newfound democracy. I propose that South Africans should have been prepared for the arrival and practice of Democracy first. For this huge blunder we have a weak FW De Klerk and an eager, over enthusiastic Nelson Mandela to blame. To rectify it a stronger, wiser and taller Leadership is required. We can never go back to correct those distant errors, but we must attempt to make things better in our life-time and that of our future generations.

Chapter 5

The Crooked Line

When the ANC government promised voters prosperity and a better life for all, one must take a moment today to review the progress of this assurance. A hope that perhaps had lingered for so long that it had lost its tenacity for holding on. Slowly it is becoming clear that the promises were not fake, but the Delivery men take home everything. Indeed, a flesh-eating animal cannot be send to deliver meat.

Formal and informal Freedom fighters who were willing to surrender their very lives as the price of freedom, had become politicians. Becoming politicians also made them rich overnight. Suddenly they were elevated above the people. Lofty ideals and promises of change were becoming a mere shadow at the glittering invitation of a life of glamour and opulence for the now elite. All they now had to do was to pretend to be advocating for the rights of the people and smile all the way to the Bank.

Is it necessary at all for the politicians of SA to earn the huge salaries with all the benefits where there are others in the Nation without a house, without any income, without employment and without food? The gap is so huge between politicians and ordinary Citizens that it is becoming a gulf. Any honest politician, if there is such a thing, would not accept the unnecessary big salaries together with all the benefits. And indeed there are multitude South Africans living or rather existing below the breadline. I had the privilege of enjoying grandiose luncheons at Parliament a few times, thinking of how privileged the life of South African politicians are as compared to that of the masses. And those famous words rang in my mind as a backdrop, "the people shall govern".

Certainly, there is nothing wrong in eating well. However, when you consume at the expense of the poor who has "elected" you to empower them through the handling of their affairs, it cannot be condoned.

The ANC Premier of Mpumalanga Ndaweni Mahlangu during 1999 defiantly said, "it was okay for politicians to lie". On behalf of his associates Mahlangu affirmed what was a reality. Having enriched himself with the partial privatization of Telkom, Smuts Ngonyama, then head of the Presidency, said, "we did not struggle to be poor", thus justifying it was okay for high ranking ANC members to sell off public sector property for their own personal gain.

As of late we have been witnessing how extravagant our leaders choose to live. We know of what is publicly exposed and that is already enough to reveal the indignant and low level of parliamentarians we have. Indeed, the better life has come, but it remains the privilege of the few. Let us have a look at these salaries.

Public office bearers earning more than 1 million rand will receive a five per cent increase and officer bearers earning less than 1 million rand will receive six per cent from April 1, 2014. This meant that President Zuma would receive about R100, 000 in back payments as his salary increased from 2.62 million rand to 2.75 million. Deputy President Cyril Ramaphosa's salary would increase from 2.47 million rand to 2.6 million. Ramaphosa is currently one of the five wealthiest black South Africans with a net worth of more than 665,659,021 million rand and it is still growing. The South African Government has just given brand-new top of the range vehicles to Traditional Leaders and kings during 2015.

Renumeration of Public Office Bearers		
Office Bearer	**From**	**To**
Ministers	R 2,1m	R 2,21m
Deputy Ministers	R 1,73m	R 1,82m
Speaker of National Parliament	R 2,47m	R 2,6m
Chief Justice	R 2,47m	R 2,6m
Member of Parliament	R 933 852	R 989 883
Premiers	R 1,98m	R 2,08m
Mayors	R 1,09m	R 1,15m
Constitutional Court judges	R 1,98m	R 2,08m
Supreme Court of Appeal judges	R 1,98m	R 2,08m
Judges in the high and labour court	R 1,61m	R 1,69m
Magistrates	R 743 542	R 788 155
Traditional kings	R 1,02m	R 1,07

The question that lingers, and rightfully so, is whether the people consequently deserve to suffer economically and physically. While in the meantime, the fat cats are indeed bloating out of their skins. How much of those unnecessary cash could not have been spent on education, housing, employment and more needed areas. At the time of the writing of this book, the electricity crisis escalates. Escom faces serious deficits, and yet the staff is receiving huge stipends and unbelievable perks. I met an Escom worker who was living in a luxury guest house and shortly after that bought the same house. Yet, in the middle of all the good life, the energy provider keep shouting, "crises!"

Have we been lied to or will it really be taking forever to eradicate the injustices of the past? President Jacob Zuma has managed to build from scratch a town for his own luxury and comfort almost overnight and yet struggles to provide something as basic as housing, education, services and employment to millions of homeless and unemployed South Africans who had been provided by that hope. Right there the situation should be summed up quite well. The current administration has indeed triggered a huge loss of respect as well as a growing mistrust in government. How can they be trusted if they were showing their inability to deliver on creating a better life for all, yet that life is lived by some? Rumours existed in 1994 already of a rigged Election. The European Union's report on the election compiled at the end of May 1994, published two years after the election, criticised the Independent Electoral Commission's lack of preparedness for the polls, the shortages of voting materials at many voting stations, and the absence of effective safeguards against fraud in the counting process. In particular it expressed disquiet that International observers were kept out at a critical stage of counting votes which leaves a big question mark on the fairness of the result. This means that both the electorate and the world were "simply left to guess at the way the final result was achieved.". The ANC then "won" 252 of the 400 seats of Parliament.

A waste of money and resources had never been so rampant as for the past twenty years in South Africa. The President with his extravagant lifestyle, had to use millions of state funds to build a village for himself. As if not enough, the administration of the flamboyant and pompous President gave him an increase from state funds. On top of already very huge salaries, top politicians unhappy with their income followed suit and unbelievably continued to incentivise themselves more including a variety of benefits. Are South Africans really that gullible?

When President Thabo Mbeki started "empowering" women by providing them top positions in the Country, it was accelerated by Mr Zuma under so-called International weight. It leaves a lot of riddled marvel, notwithstanding that some indeed deserved the roles they play, or do they?

President Zuma had been insulted when called less than honourable by fellow-politicians, as well as ordinary folks, and yet he could not be hindered in the least. I admitted to acquaintances that I had never seen anybody this arrogant, whilst facing criminal and scandalous charges, he looked at television cameras from local and abroad and did not waver. At first I thought it to be a strange kind of almost admirable strength, but when the actions of the man continued, degraded the Country and mocked the poor and homeless masses, I had to sit up and see it for what it was, a demonic forte.

Could the burden of expense of the ANC, not have been better spent on important issues such as proper Housing, Employment, Education, Safety, Security, Water and Electricity and Infra-structure. Why do the citizens of the Land should be paying for the excessive parties, disproportionate events and bribery of others? The nation only recently heard reliably through the international media about the ten million USD paid to FIFA as agreed to by the former President Thabo Mbeki.

The meagre Housing units offered to some South Africans should not be the norm. Surely if the Country can afford a luxury palace with servants for a king of one group and a Nkandla for Mr Zuma, then we deserve better housing.

Education has become almost unattainable due to costs. This had become a huge discouraging factor especially amongst Youth. Parents who so much desire for their children to study and become professionals are unable to assist them because it is just too expensive. Bursaries even as offered by Government are not enough.

In recent revelations, two ANC senior Cadres were exposed as having falsely impersonated themselves as doctors. Those cases quickly caught the dark sea of forgetfulness, as so many crimes perpetrated by ANC members do. The way in which the Department of Education is managed, tempts one somewhat to throw suspicion on the qualifications of "Doctor" Blade Ndzimandi.

The statement that all people shall be equal before the law, has been proven to be an empty saying. The president of the Republic of South Africa has been a blatant criminal who successfully managed to evade the justice system of his Country. One sometimes cannot but wonder what would have happened to him - with all he perpetrated - had he not been president or a very important ANC Cader. (VIAC).

Chapter 6

Forward: Crooked or straight Line

Plato, tells us "tyranny arises, as a rule, from democracy". Historically, this process has occurred in three quite different ways. Before describing the several patterns of social change, let us state precisely what is meant by "democracy."

Pondering the question of "Who should rule," the democrat gives his answer: "the majority of politically equal citizens, either in person or through their representatives." In other words, equality and majority rule are the two fundamental principles of democracy. A democracy may be either liberal or illiberal.

Genuine liberalism is the answer to an entirely different question: How should government be exercised? The answer it provides is: regardless of who rules, government must be carried out in such a way that each person enjoys the greatest amount of freedom, compatible with the common good. This means that an absolute monarchy could be liberal (but hardly democratic) and a democracy could be totalitarian, illiberal, and tyrannical, with a majority brutally persecuting minorities. (We are, of course, using the term "liberal" in the globally accepted version and not in the American sense, which since the New Deal has been totally perverted.)

How could a democracy, even an initially liberal one, develop into a totalitarian tyranny? As we said in the beginning, there are three avenues of approach, and in each case the evolution would be of an "organic" nature. The tyranny would evolve from the very character of even a liberal democracy because there is, from the beginning, a worm in the apple: freedom and equality do not mix, they practically exclude each other. Equality doesn't exist in nature and therefore can be established only by force. He who wants geographic equality must dynamite mountains and fill up the valleys. To get a hedge of even height one should apply pruning shears. To achieve equal scholastic levels in a school one would have to pressure certain students into extra hard work while holding back others.

The first road to totalitarian tyranny (though by no means the most frequently used) is the overthrow by force of a liberal democracy through a revolutionary movement, as a rule a party advocating tyranny but unable to win the necessary support in free elections. The stage for such violence is set if the parties represent philosophies so different as to make dialogue and compromise impossible. Carl von Clausewitz said "wars are the continuation of diplomacy by other means, and in ideologically divided nations revolutions are truly the continuation of parliamentarism with other means". The result is the absolute rule of one "party" which, having finally achieved complete control, might still call itself a party, referring to its parliamentary past, when it still was merely a part of the diet.

A typical case is the Red October of 1917. The Bolshevik wing of the Russian Social Democratic Workers' Party could not win the elections in Alexander Kerenski's democratic Russian Republic and therefore staged a coup with the help of a defeated, marauding army and navy, and in this way established a firm socialistic tyranny. Many liberal democracies are enfeebled by party strife to such an extent that revolutionary organizations can easily seize power, and sometimes the citizenry, for a time, seems happy that chaos has come to an end. In Italy, the Marcia su Roma of the Fascists made them the rulers of the country. Mussolini, a socialist of old, had learned the technique of political conquest from his International Socialist friends and, not surprisingly, Fascist Italy was the second European power, after Laborite Britain (and long before the United States) to recognize the Soviet regime.

The second avenue toward totalitarian tyranny is "free elections." It can happen that a totalitarian party with great popularity gains such momentum and so many votes that it becomes legally and democratically a country's master. This happened in Germany in 1932 when no less than sixty per cent of the electorate voted for totalitarian despotism: for every two National Socialists, there was one international socialist in the form of a Marxist Communist, and another one in the form of a somewhat less Marxist Social Democrat. Under these circumstances liberal democracy was doomed, since it had no longer a majority in the Reichstag. This development could have been halted only by a military dictatorship (as envisaged by General Von Schleicher who was later murdered by the Nazis) or by a restoration of the Hohenzollerns (as planned by Bruning). Yet, within the democratic and constitutional framework, the National Socialists were bound to win.

How did the "Nazis" manage to win in this way? The answer is simple: being a mass movement striving for a parliamentary majority, they singled out unpopular minorities (the smaller, the better) and then rallied popular support against them. The National Socialist Workers' Party was "a popular movement based on exact science" (Hitler's words), militating against the hated few: The Jews, the nobility, the rich, the clergy, the modern artists, the "intellectuals," categories frequently overlapping, and finally against the mentally handicapped and the Gypsies. National Socialism was the "legal revolt" of the common man against the uncommon, of the "people" (Volk) against privileged and therefore envied and hated groups. Remember that Lenin, Mussolini, and Hitler called their rule "democratic"—demokratiya po novomu, democrazia organizzata, deutsche Demokratie—but they never dared to call it "liberal" in the worldwide (non-American) sense.

Carl Schmitt, in his 93rd year, analysed this evolution in a famous essay entitled "The Legal World Revolution": "this sort of revolu-tion-the German Revolution of 1933-simply comes about through the ballot and can happen in any country where a party pledged to totalitarian rule gains a relative or absolute majority and thus takes over the government 'democratically'". Plato gave an account of such a procedure which fits, with the fidelity of a Xerox copy, the constitutional transition in Germany: there is the "popular leader" who takes to heart the interest of the "simple people," of the "ordinary, decent fellow" against the crafty rich. He is widely acclaimed by the many and builds up a body guard only to protect himself and, of course, the interests of the "people".

Chapter 7

In the Name of the People

Think of Hitler's SA and SS, as well as of the tendency to apply
wherever possible the prefix Volk (people): Volkswagen (people's car),
Volksempfänger (people's radio set), des ge-sunde Volksempfinden (the
healthy sentiments of the people), Volksgericht (people's law court).
Needless to say, this verbal policy continues in the "German Democratic
Republic" where we see a "People's Police," a "People's Army," while
Moscow's satellite states are called "People's Democracies."

All this implies that in earlier times only the elites had a chance to
govern and that now, at long last, the common man is the master of his
destiny able to enjoy the good things in life! It matters little that the
realities are quite different. A very high-ranking Soviet official recently
said to a European prince: "Your ancestors exploited the people,
claiming that they ruled by the Grace of God, but we are doing much
better, we exploit the people in the name of the people."

Then there is the third way in which a democracy changes into a
totalitarian tyranny. The first political analyst who foresaw this hitherto-
never-experienced kind of evolution was Alexis de Tocqueville. He drew
an exact and frightening picture of our Provider State (wrongly called
Welfare State) in the second volume of his Democracy in America,
published in 1835; he spoke at length about a form of tyranny which he
could only describe, but not name, because it had no historic precedent.
Admittedly, it took several generations until Tocqueville's vision became
a reality.

He envisioned a democratic government in which nearly all human affairs would be controlled by a mild, "compassionate" but determined government under which the citizens would practise their pursuit of happiness as "timid animals", losing all initiative and freedom. "The Roman Emperors", he said, "could direct their wrath against individuals, but control of all forms of life was out of the question under their rule". We should add that in Tocqueville's time the technology for such a surveillance and regulation was inadequately developed. The computer had not been invented and thus his warnings found little echo in the past century.

Tocqueville, a genuine liberal and legitimist, had gone to America not only because he was concerned with trends in the United States, but also because the electoral victory of Andrew Jackson. He was the first Democrat in the White House and the man who introduced the highly democratic Spoils System, a genuine invitation to corruption. The Founding Fathers, as Charles Beard has pointed out, hated democracy more than Original Sin. But now a French ideology, only too familiar to Tocqueville, had started to conquer America.

This portentous development lured the French aristocrat to the New World where he wanted to observe the global advance of "democratism," in his opinion and to his dismay bound to penetrate everywhere and to end in either anarchy or the New Tyranny—which he referred to as "democratic despotism." The road to anarchy is more apt to be taken by South Europeans and South Americans (and it usually terminates in military dictatorships in order to prevent total dissolution). The northern nations on the other hand, while keeping all democratic appearances, tend to founder in totalitarian welfare bureaucracy. The lack of a common political philosophy is more conducive to the development of outright revolutions in the South where civil wars tend to be "the continuation of meeting with others (and more violent) in a legislature means", while the North is rather given to evolutionary processes, to a creeping increase of slavery and a decrease of personal freedom and initiative. This process can be much more paralysing than a mere personal dictatorship, military or otherwise, without an ideological and totalitarian character. The Franco and Salazar regimes and certain Latin American authoritarian governments, all softening with the years, are good examples.

Chapter 8

Toward Servitude

Tocqueville did not tell us just how the gradual change toward totalitarian servitude can come about. But 150 years ago, he could not exactly foresee that the parliamentary scene would produce two main types of parties: The Santa Claus parties, predominantly on the Left, and the Tighten-Your-Belt parties, on the Right. The Santa Claus parties, with presents for the many, normally take from some people to give to others: they operate with largesse, to use the term of John Adams. Socialism, whether national or international, will act in the name of "distributive justice," as well as "social justice" and "progress," and thus gain popularity. You don't, after all, shoot Santa Claus. Thus, these parties normally win elections, and politicians who use their slogans are effective vote-getters.

The Tighten-Your-Belt parties, if they unexpectedly gain power, generally act more wisely, but they rarely have the courage to undo the policies of the Santa parties. The voting masses, who frequently favour the Santa parties, would retract their support if the Tighten-Your-Belt parties were to act radically and consistently. Profligates are usually more popular than misers. In fact, the Santa Claus parties are rarely utterly defeated, but they sometimes defeat themselves by featuring hopeless candidates or causing political turmoil or economic disaster.

A politicised Saint Nicholas is a grim taskmaster. Gifts cannot be distributed without bureaucratic regulation, registration, and regimentation of the entire country. Countless strings are attached to the gifts received from "above". The State interferes in all domains of human existence—education, health, transportation, communication, entertainment, food, commerce, industry, farming, building, employment, inheritance, social life, birth, and death.

There are two aspects to this large-scale interference: statism and equal opportunity, yet they are fundamentally connected since to regiment the social order perfectly, you must reduce people to an equal level. Thus, a "classless society" becomes the real aim, and every kind of discrimination must come to an end. But, discrimination is fundamental to a free life, because freedom of will and choice is a characteristic of man and his personality. If I marry Bess instead of Jean, I obviously discriminate against Jean; if I employ Dr. Nishiyama as a teacher of Japanese instead of Dr. O'Hanrahan, I discriminate against the latter, and so forth. (One should not be surprised if an opera house that rejects a 4-foot tall Bambuti singer for the role of Siegfried in Wagner's "Ring" is accused of racism!)

There is, in fact, only either just or unjust discrimination. Yet, classless democracy remains adamant in its totalitarian policy. The popular pastime of modern democracies of punishing the diligent and thrifty, while rewarding the lazy, improvident, and unthrifty, is cultivated via the State, fulfilling a demo-egali-tarian programme based on a demo-totalitarian ideology.

Democratic tyranny, evolving on the sly as a slow and subtle corruption leading to total State control, is thus the third and by no means rarest road to the most modern form of slavery.

Chapter 9

Conclusion

A Government of National Unity did not work; the current government has failed too. Only a government of the people by the people and for the people will work. This is the supposed definition of democracy. How come that we cannot apply this form of Government, which is preferred by most Countries in the world? Is it preferred because of the loophole it holds for corruption to succeed in peace? A Government elected free and fair without the interference of any other powers. I suggest Mr Zuma and his inner circle must be arrested, the current regime must be replaced by intermediate military rule in preparation of free and fair elections.

Are we free? Are we economically free? If we were, can we afford where to live, what to eat and when to eat? Are we free to access Education, essential services and proper housing? If you think these goals are far-fetched, have a look at our politicians. From the smallest parties in Parliament to the majority, the Line is Crooked.

It is indeed time for the people of South Africa to rise and take what belong to them. The demand for the delivery of our freedom is long overdue. So, let us not fear! Let us march onward to government, save our Country and our government before the Republic of South Africa become yet another statistic of dark Africa.

It is time to replace the unqualified Architect drawing skew lines on the canvass of our Land of birth and promise. Time to allow a skilled and experienced hand to draw a straight Line erasing the Crooked Line.

On April 1st 2016, finally the Nation set up in expectation on the announcement by the South African Broadcasting Network that the President will appear on national television for a special announcement. This following a meeting with the top six leaders of the African National Congress, shortly after the rule of the Constitutional Court that the President is guilty of spending State Funds for non-security upgrades at his private residence at Nkandla. Almost everyone expected him to do the honourable thing, but he played South Africans once again with a cleverly written speech, but no resignation. The dishonourable President of the Republic of South Africa remains in power yet another day. Viva ANC Viva!

Addendum A:

About the Freedom Charter

The Freedom Charter was the statement of core principles of the South African Congress Alliance, which consisted of the African National Congress and its allies the South African Indian Congress, the South African Congress of Democrats and the Coloured People's Congress. It is characterized by its opening demand; The People Shall Govern!

In 1955, the ANC sent out fifty thousand volunteers countrywide to collect 'freedom demands' from the people of South Africa. This system was designed to give all South Africans equal rights. Demands such as "Land to be given to all landless people", "Living wages and shorter hours of work", "Free and compulsory education, irrespective of colour, race or nationality" were synthesised into the final document by ANC leaders including Z.K. Mathews and Lionel 'Rusty' Bernstein.

The Charter was officially adopted on June 26, 1955 at a Congress of the People in Kliptown. The meeting was attended by roughly three thousand delegates, but was broken up by police on the second day, although by then the charter had been read in full. The crowd had shouted its approval of each section with cries of 'Afrika!' and 'Mayibuye!'

The document is notable for its demand for and commitment to a non-racial South Africa, this remains the platform of the ANC. The charter also calls for democracy and human rights, land reform, labour rights, and nationalization. After the congress was denounced as treason by the South African government. The ANC was banned and 156 activists were arrested, including Nelson Mandela who was first imprisoned in 1962. However, the charter continued to circulate in the underground and inspired a generation of young militants.

On February 11 1990, Nelson Mandela was finally freed and the ANC came to power after the first democratic elections were held in South Africa in April 1994. The new Constitution of South Africa included in its text many of the demands called for in the Freedom Charter. Nearly all the enumerated concerns regarding equality of race and language were directly addressed in the constitution, although the document included nothing to the effect of the nationalisation of industry or redistribution of land, both of which were specifically outlined in the charter.

The Tripartite Alliance

The ANC is in an alliance with the South African Communist Party (SACP) and the Congress of South African Trade Unions (COSATU). Each Alliance partner is an independent organisation with its own constitution, membership and programmes. The Alliance is founded on a common commitment to the objectives of the National Democratic Revolution, and the need to unite the largest possible cross-section of South Africans behind these objectives.

•Former Leaders

•The Officials

John Dube

Sefako Makgatho

Zaccheus Mahabane

Josiah Gumede

Pixley Seme

Alfred Xuma

James Moroka

Albert Luthuli

Oliver Tambo

Nelson Mandela

Govan Mbeki

Walter Sisulu

Thabo Mbeki

President: Jacob Zuma

Deputy President: Cyril Ramaphosa

National Chairperson: Baleka Mbete

Secretary General: Gwede Mantashe

Deputy Secretary General: Jessie Duarte

Treasurer General: Zweli Mkhize

Addendum B:

The Freedom Charter

As adopted at the Congress of the People, Kliptown, on 26 June 1955

We, the People of South Africa, declare for all our country and the world to know:

- that South Africa belongs to all who live in it, black and white, and that no government can justly claim authority unless it is based on the will of all the people;

- that our people have been robbed of their birth right to land, liberty and peace by a form of government founded on injustice and inequality;

- that our country will never be prosperous or free until all our people live in brotherhood, enjoying equal rights and opportunities;

- that only a democratic state, based on the will of all the people, can secure to all their birth right without distinction of colour, race, sex or belief;

And therefore, we, the people of South Africa, black and white together equals, countrymen and brothers adopt this Freedom Charter;

And we pledge ourselves to strive together, sparing neither strength nor courage, until the democratic changes here set out have been won.

The People Shall Govern!

Every man and woman shall have the right to vote for and to stand as a candidate for all bodies which make laws;

All people shall be entitled to take part in the administration of the country;

The rights of the people shall be the same, regardless of race, colour or sex;

All bodies of minority rule, advisory boards, councils and authorities shall be replaced by democratic organs of self-government.

All National Groups Shall have Equal Rights!

There shall be equal status in the bodies of state, in the courts and in the schools for all national groups and races;

All people shall have equal right to use their own languages, and to develop their own folk culture and customs;

All national groups shall be protected by law against insults to their race and national pride;

The preaching and practice of national, race or colour discrimination and contempt shall be a punishable crime;

All apartheid laws and practices shall be set aside.

The People Shall Share in the Country`s Wealth!

The national wealth of our country, the heritage of South Africans, shall be restored to the people;

The mineral wealth beneath the soil, the Banks and monopoly industry shall be transferred to the ownership of the people;

All other industry and trade shall be controlled to assist the wellbeing of the people;

All people shall have equal rights to trade where they choose, to manufacture and to enter all trades, crafts and professions.

The Land Shall Be Shared Among Those Who Work It!

Restrictions of land ownership on a racial basis shall be ended, and all the land re-divided amongst those who work it to banish famine and land hunger;

The state shall help the peasants with implements, seed, tractors and dams to save the soil and assist the tillers;

Freedom of movement shall be guaranteed to all who work on the land;

All shall have the right to occupy land wherever they choose;

People shall not be robbed of their cattle, and forced labour and farm prisons shall be abolished.

All shall be Equal before the Law!

No-one shall be imprisoned, deported or restricted without a fair trial; No-one shall be condemned by the order of any Government official;

The courts shall be representative of all the people;

Imprisonment shall be only for serious crimes against the people, and shall aim at re-education, not vengeance;

The police force and army shall be open to all on an equal basis and shall be the helpers and protectors of the people;

All laws which discriminate on grounds of race, colour or belief shall be repealed.

All Shall Enjoy Equal Human Rights!

The law shall guarantee to all their right to speak, to organise, to meet, to publish, to preach, to worship and to educate their children;

The privacy of the house from police raids shall be protected by law;

All shall be free to travel without restriction from countryside to town, from province to province, and from South Africa abroad;

Pass Laws, permits and all other laws restricting these freedoms shall be abolished.

There Shall Be Work and Security!

All who work shall be free to form trade unions, to elect their officers and to make wage agreements with their employers;

The state shall recognise the right and duty of all to work, and to draw full unemployment benefits;

Men and women of all races shall receive equal pay for equal work;

There shall be a forty-hour working week, a national minimum wage, paid annual leave, and sick leave for all workers, and maternity leave on full pay for all working mothers;

Miners, domestic workers, farm workers and civil servants shall have the same rights as all others who work;

Child labour, compound labour, the tot system and contract labour shall be abolished.

The Doors of Learning and Culture Shall Be Opened!

The government shall discover, develop and encourage national talent for the enhancement of our cultural life;

All the cultural treasures of mankind shall be open to all, by free exchange of books, ideas and contact with other lands;

The aim of education shall be to teach the youth to love their people and their culture, to honour human brotherhood, liberty and peace;

Education shall be free, compulsory, universal and equal for all children; Higher education and technical training shall be opened to all by means of state allowances and scholarships awarded based on merit;

Adult illiteracy shall be ended by a mass state education plan;

Teachers shall have all the rights of other citizens;

The colour bar in cultural life, in sport and in education shall be abolished.

There Shall Be Houses, Security and Comfort!

All people shall have the right to live where they choose, be decently housed, and to bring up their families in comfort and security;

Unused housing space to be made available to the people;

Rent and prices shall be lowered, food plentiful and no-one shall go hungry;

A preventive health scheme shall be run by the state;

Free medical care and hospitalisation shall be provided for all, with special care for mothers and young children;

Slums shall be demolished, and new suburbs built where all have transport, roads, lighting, playing fields, crèches and social centres;

The aged, the orphans, the disabled and the sick shall be cared for by the state;

Rest, leisure and recreation shall be the right of all:

Fenced locations and ghettoes shall be abolished, and laws which break up families shall be repealed.

There Shall be Peace and Friendship!

South Africa shall be a fully independent state which respects the rights and sovereignty of all nations;

South Africa shall strive to maintain world peace and the settlement of all international disputes by negotiation - not war;

Peace and friendship amongst all our people shall be secured by upholding the equal rights, opportunities and status of all;

The people of the protectorates Basutoland, Bechuanaland and Swaziland shall be free to decide for themselves their own future;

The right of all peoples of Africa to independence and self-government shall be recognised, and shall be the basis of close co-operation.

Let all people who love their people and their country now say, as we say here:

THESE FREEDOMS WE WILL FIGHT FOR, SIDE BY SIDE, THROUGHOUT OUR LIVES, UNTIL WE HAVE WON OUR LIBERTY

Bibiliography

McKinley, D.T. (2012) 'Of Flowers and Thorns: Where has the 'Public' Gone in Public Service?', http://SACSIS.org.za.

Fischer, A. (2014) ""Democracy as We Know It Is a Tyranny of the Majority". http://panampost.com/belen-marty/2014/10/10/hana-fischer-democracy-as-we-know-it-is-a-tyranny-of-the-majority/#

http://www.timeslive.co.za/politics/zumaandministerssalariesincreaseTimesLIVE.htm

http://www.timeslive.co.za /ThefiverichestblackSouthAfricansa